BASTIEN LEPAGE

LECTOR HOUSE PUBLIC DOMAIN WORKS

BASTIEN LEPAGE

FRANÇOIS CRASTRE,
FREDERIC TABER COOPER,
M. HENRY ROUJON

ISBN: 978-93-90294-62-6

Published: 1914

LECTOR HOUSE LLP
E-MAIL: lectorpublishing@gmail.com

PLATE I.—THE SONG OF SPRINGTIME

(Museum at Verdun)

This is one of the artist's earliest works. A certain embarrassment may be noted in the manner in which the Cupids are treated; even at this period, it is easy to see that allegory is not suited to the precise and realistic talent of this painter; yet the young girl is designed with a vigour which already foreshadows the masterly art of Hay-making.

MASTERPIECES IN COLOUR

BASTIEN LEPAGE
(1848-1884)

BY

FR. CRASTRE

TRANSLATED FROM THE FRENCH BY FREDERIC TABER COOPER

EDITED BY
M. HENRY ROUJON

ILLUSTRATED WITH EIGHT
REPRODUCTIONS IN COLOUR

1914

CONTENTS

LIST OF ILLUSTRATIONS

BASTIEN LEPAGE

There are certain beings who bear the stamp of the divine seal and are preordained to receive the highest favours within the gift of glory; they are fated to pass through life like those brilliant meteors which are seen to flash across the heavens and disappear in the same instant. Bastien-Lepage was one of these meteors. But while the others leave behind them only a luminous trail that swiftly vanishes, this rare artist, snatched so prematurely from the field of art, traced his passage in a furrow of dazzling splendour, the radiance of which has not even yet begun to fade.

Bastien-Lepage was a painter in the noblest acceptation of the term; it may even be asserted that he would have exercised considerable influence upon the art of his epoch if Destiny had not stupidly mown down the sturdy flower of his genius in the very hour of its brightest blossoming. Born into this world with a solid tenacity of purpose which seems to be a special gift of the soil of Lorraine to her sons and daughters, he had a clear-cut and unalterable conception of what painting should be. His mind was receptive only of simple ideas, his eye perceived only visions that were tangible, such as were unobscured by any shadow or any artifice. He was the apostle of clearness, both in conception and in execution. Every time that he tried experimentally to turn aside from his chosen path, he ceased to be himself, he fell below his own standards. What interested him most of all, in the life of this world which he observed so eagerly, as though he had a presentiment of his early end, was nature's most precise and most uncompromising manifestation, both in line and in relief; namely, the peasant and the environment which frames him. Having deliberately chosen such models, Bastien-Lepage could not pretend to be the painter of the Beautiful, nor did he ever become so. He did not even adorn his subjects with that special sort of idealism with which Millet embellished even his most uncouth rustic types, a slightly melancholy idealism obtained by a sombre toning down of colour, which Bastien-Lepage held in horror. His peasants stand out boldly, in the crude glare of flamboyant noontide, under a summer sun that refuses to leave hidden any part of their ugliness or their defects. He painted them as he saw them, with the searching rays striking them full in the face; and his brush was a stranger to any compromise, intolerant of even the slightest betterment, in the course of the literal transference of his model to his canvas. It made no difference how handsome or how homely a given subject might be, Bastien-Lepage would always render him precisely as nature, in a grudging or indulgent mood, had made him,—that is to say, truly and sincerely, with a precision that would be almost photographic, if the minuteness of his technique were not ennobled by the high quality of his art. With such gifts, Bastien-Lepage was foreordained to be a marvellous interpreter of rural life, and such he was in the highest degree; in like manner, he could not fail to become a portrait painter of the first order, and it was in this capacity also that he enrolled himself among the most interesting and vigorous artists of our epoch.

PLATE II.—PORTRAIT OF M. WALLON

(Museum at Verdun)

Few artists have been able to endow their models with such an animated expression of life. All the keenness, intelligence and austerity of this prominent personage, known by the name of Father of the Constitution, are eloquently transferred to this page, with a sobriety of means that still further emphasizes its vigour.

HIS YOUTH

Jules Bastien-Lepage was born at Damvillers, in the department of the Meuse, on the first of November, 1848. His parents were of the well-to-do farming class, occupied from one year's end to the other with the work of the fields. Consequently, all the early boyhood of the artist was passed in daily contact with the soil of Lorraine and with the sons of that soil. He knew them, one and all, in his native village; he grew up among them; he went to school side by side with the other little rustics of his own age: he understood the peasant class, with all their faults, their virtues, their habits of life; he learned to read in their faces, which were a sealed book to the outsider, the opinions and emotions which they had in common with him.

These childhood impressions were destined to abide with him throughout his life; he cherished to the end a fervent love for his native land, and he felt that he had an infinitely noble task in painting that life of the fields which the Second Empire affected to despise.

But though he came of peasant stock, it was Bastien-Lepage's good fortune that these same peasants were in prosperous circumstances and could afford to give him an education. They were ambitious for him; and it hurt them to see their little Jules, who was so wide-awake, so intelligent, and at the same time so frail, leading the hard and monotonous life of the fields, following the plough, tilling the soil. It needed only a few household economies to enable him to continue his studies; so, when the time came, young Bastien-Lepage wended his way towards Verdun, where he entered upon his college course.

There is nothing that marks in any particular way these years of study, nothing to indicate that the boy was a youthful prodigy, nor that he showed any special aptitude for drawing. But he was studious, diligent, and anxious to avoid reprimands and to fulfil the expectations of his parents. In due time he obtained his bachelor's degree, which at that period was highly prized. His father, filled with pride, already began to form brilliant projects for his future, already foresaw him a distinguished official, supervising some great branch of the public service. As a matter of fact, a position was found for the young baccalaureate in a government department which was neither the most desirable nor the one of least importance; namely, the Post Office Department. Bastien-Lepage was not vastly delighted with the choice, but, dutiful son that he was, he accepted the modest clerkship offered him. One circumstance contributed, in a large degree, towards overcoming his reluctance: the post assigned to him from the start was in Paris, of which he had often heard marvellous things, and in which he hoped that he would be able to follow his secret inclination. For, in the interval his vocation had revealed itself; he had conceived a passion for drawing, for colouring, for painting; and, like Correggio, he was eager to say in his turn, "I too am a painter!"

Accordingly he set forth, leaving behind him no suspicion of his purpose. Upon arriving at the capital, he acquitted himself scrupulously of his official duties, but every leisure moment was consecrated to visiting the museums and exhibitions. He saturated himself with the wealth of beauty strewn broadcast through the Louvre, and was thrilled with admiration at contact with the masters of every school and country. He did not care equally for them all, in spite of their genius; his intimate preferences leaned to the side of Flemish rather than Italian art; but he was not insensible to the lofty inspiration, the severe harmony, the faultless composition, which have made the great masters of the Renaissance the most astonishing prodigies in the history of painting.

But while the older schools of art delighted him, he followed with no less attention the movement of contemporary painting. At the hour when his critical spirit awoke, certain new elements and new formulas had come to light and had been put into practice by two audacious and gifted artists by the names of Courbet and Manet. Although the prolonged struggle between the classicists and romanticists had not yet come to an end, these two rival schools were entrenched in their positions and refused to stir forth from them. Supporters of Delacroix and of Ingres confined themselves strictly to their respective hostile formulas, doing nothing either to expand or to rejuvenate them. Whoever dared to venture outside of one of these two beaten tracks was regarded as a madman, and his attempts were greeted with derisive clamours by both parties, who declared a momentary truce, for the purpose of annihilating him by a joint attack. Courbet, who was scorned by Ingres, met with equally harsh criticism from Delacroix; and as for Manet, he had managed to call down universal wrath upon his head, and at the Salon of 1863 it became necessary to place his *Olympia* in the very topmost line upon the wall, in order to protect it from the fury of the public, hounded on by the hue and cry of the critics.

Bastien-Lepage made mental notes of all the episodes of this struggle; he listened to the criticisms and passed them through the crucible of his unspoiled mind, in the presence of the very works under indictment. His good sense showed him how large an element of injustice entered into these hostilities. Moreover, his peasant blood inclined him to sympathize with those artists who refused to bind themselves to seek for beauty only within the limits of academic form, and who had the ability to make it flash forth from the humblest and even the most vulgar type of subject. Furthermore, this constant study of matters pertaining to art, day by day added fuel to the hidden fire smouldering within him; he was conscious of its mounting flame. Back of the rude sketches, drawn and coloured in the tiny chamber befitting an humble postal clerk, he perceived vaguely that he also possessed the temperament of a painter, and little by little he witnessed the unfolding of his artist's soul.

PLATE III.—THE ARTIST'S MOTHER

(Collection of É. Bastien-Lepage)

What a kindly and gentle face this is, the face of the woman to whom the artist applied the tender endearment of "Good little mother"! In this work, it is evident that the heart guided the hand of the painter. None but a son could have rendered with such emotion the humid tenderness of those eyes and the maternal caress of those lips. It is a powerful work, which enrolls Bastien-Lepage in the foremost rank of portrait painters.

At last, unable to bear it longer, he resigned from the postal service and enrolled his name at the Beaux-Arts. At this time, when he entered the studio of Cabanel, he was but little more than nineteen years of age. Cabanel, to be sure, was not the painter of his choice, but Bastien-Lepage was not for that reason any the less appreciative of a system of instruction which was dominated by a worship of line-work. His training under Cabanel was not without value to the young artist, who throughout his life, even in his most realistic paintings, proved himself to be an impeccable master of design.

At the outset, however, he was beset with difficulties. Now that his salary as a postal clerk had ceased and remittances from the family were necessarily restricted, Bastien-Lepage exerted himself to gain a living by his own efforts. He had no lack of courage, and he had in addition that Lorraine tenacity which enabled him to confront all difficulties with tranquil assurance. He worked with desperate energy, and in the intervals of respite from his labours he overran all Paris in search of orders from business houses. It was an inglorious task, but at least it enabled him to live; thus it happened that about 1873 he produced a widely circulated advertisement for a perfumery house. Up to this time he had remained wholly unknown; and although he had already exhibited one painting, at the Salon of 1870, it was passed by unheeded both by the critics and the general public.

This lack of success in no wise discouraged him, for he had faith. It was in the year 1874 that he exhibited *The Song of Springtime*. It was a veritable revelation. There was no neglect this time. The public gathered in throngs before his canvas, and the critics, notwithstanding a few objections to details, were lavish in their praise and hailed him as having the qualities of a true artist. Naturally, the picture was not perfect, but it well merited the flattering reception which it received. In a springtime landscape a young peasant girl is seated beneath a tree, looking before her over a sunlit plain. Around her skirts a whole bevy of Cupids are gathering blossoms and offering them to the girl. Here, at the first stroke, is an assertion of the young painter's independence, his formal determination to emancipate himself from the accepted formulas in his treatment of the eternal theme of a young girl's soul, opening to the first appeal of love. As a matter of fact, the allegory is somewhat clumsy; you realize that the author's talent does not run to sentimental compositions. Yet the young girl is brushed in with an energetic hand, and all that rather coarse robustness that distinguishes the women of peasant stock is blended in a masterly manner with the naïve innocence of simple souls. *The Song of Springtime* was Bastien-Lepage's first attempt in that vein of realistic painting in which he was soon destined to excel.

That same year he produced *Grandfather's Portrait*, which also attracted much attention. The artist had placed his model in the little garden adjoining the home of his birth. This portrait, which belongs to-day to the painter's brother, is remarkable for its naturalness, its touch of intimate understanding, and its vigour of execution.

Bastien-Lepage had now acquired a name. His *Song of Springtime* won him a third class medal, and the State purchased the painting for the museum at Verdun, where it at present hangs.

In the following year he exhibited *Her First Communion*, picturing a young and pretty country girl, stiff and self-conscious under her white veil. This work was the product of keen observation, and is deliberately stilted and traditional in its style of execution, recalling in some measure the French primitive school. Bastien-Lepage evidently had in mind the portraits by François Cluet: his little communicant is infinitely artificial in her spotless finery, yet infinitely alive under the thin surface wash of colour which recalls the *Elizabeth of Austria*, wife of Charles IX, as painted by the greatest of the French primitives.

Simultaneously with this picture he exhibited the *Portrait of M. Hayem*, in which the vigorous treatment of the face, with its clear, firm colour tones and sober workmanship, proclaimed him already a portrait painter of the first order.

His success this time was more marked: he received a medal of the second class. A less modest artist would have allowed himself to be borne tranquilly along by the mounting tide of glory; but Bastien-Lepage did not yet feel that he was sufficiently sure of himself. He wished to continue for a while longer, working, learning, perfecting himself; he even conceived the idea, in spite of his renown, of competing for the *Prix de Rome*. Accordingly, the painter of *The Song of Springtime* and *Her First Communion* might shortly after have been seen entering the lists like any ordinary nobody. He obtained only the second prize.

He presented himself again the following year, but with no better success. The subject assigned for the competition was *Priam at the Feet of Achilles*. It is easy to understand that such a theme was little calculated to inspire an artist of Bastien-Lepage's temperament; he found it impossible to attain full development unless in the presence of nature herself. No amount of manual dexterity can take the place of inborn faith, and the young artist had no faith in antiquity; he never could muster any enthusiasm for the Greek or Roman gods, nor for historic scenes in which the very attitudes are dictated by the rules and regulations of time-honoured tradition.

Nevertheless, the work is not without merit; it is forceful, its colouring is good, and it falls short of perfection only in failing to conform sufficiently with what we know of ancient life. This painting is at present to be found in the Museum at Lille.

This rebuff did not discourage Bastien-Lepage unreasonably; but he decided to confine himself in the future to painting portraits and picturing the life of the fields.

HIS BEST YEARS

The same year that he failed for the second time in the competition for the *Prix de Rome*, Bastien-Lepage painted *The Portrait of M. Wallon*, which is one of his most important works as a portrait painter. In spite of its tendency towards naturalism, this canvas was nevertheless still conceived in accordance with the established technique, and the keen and serious visage of the Father of the Constitution standing out against its sombre background is a fine study in chiaroscuro.

But the following year he struck the naturalistic note more strongly in his *Portrait of Lady L.*, the only full-length, life-sized portrait that he ever painted; and he declared himself plainly and definitely a realist in his picture entitled *My Parents*. It would be impossible to find two figures more life-like, more literal, or painted with greater sincerity. This canvas amounted to a declaration of principles; for an artist whom filial piety cannot turn aside from the truth will never make sacrifices to convention: he will never consent to embellish or idealize his models through tricks of his craft; he will paint them as he sees them, without correcting any of the imperfections and ugliness with which nature has afflicted them. How clearly we recognize that these likenesses of Bastien-Lepage's parents are absolutely true to life, and how much better we like them as they are, in the simple intimacy of daily life, than if they had been decked out, all spick and span, as a less scrupulous artist would inevitably have shown them to us!

Bastien-Lepage's brother, himself a painter of some talent, has preserved in his studio at Neuilly a certain number of the artist's works, which he surrounds with pious care and feelingly exhibits to occasional visitors. The family portraits are there, pulsating with life and radiating that generous peasant kindliness which finds expression in a broad and tender smile. The father, seated in a chair in his garden, an old man with shrewd yet friendly eyes, seems so real, so actual, that we almost expect him to step down from his frame to bid us welcome. And what a marvel the *Portrait of my Mother* is, which forms a companion piece on the same wall! A somewhat wistful charm pervades this face, with its deeply graven lines, and an infinite tenderness, a true mother's tenderness, hovers over the thin, pale lips.

PLATE IV—HAY-MAKING

(Museum of the Luxembourg)

A masterpiece of contemporary painting, because of the truth of its attitudes and the vigour of its execution. It would be impossible to render
more forcibly the blissfulness of rest when the body has been racked by
the exhausting labour of the soil. In this picture, Bastien-Lepage revealed
himself as an incomparable painter of rural life.

Perhaps this is the moment, in the presence of these pictures, to emphasize
Bastien-Lepage's great value as a colourist. Few contemporary painters have used
colour with so much tact, such veritable mastery as he. Others have employed
more dazzling tonal schemes and have achieved more gorgeous effects, but no

one has rendered with such exact truth the tints of the flesh, the grayish folds of wrinkles, the profound light of the eye. And his colour is always clear, always unmistakably employed to produce a sought-after effect. There is no artifice, no trick-work, it is all straightforward, honest, precise; the opposition of light and shade never result in opacity, bitumen plays no part in his canvases, the astonishing relief of which is obtained by means of such perfect simplicity that it recalls the inimitable technique of Correggio.

In 1878 he exhibited *Hay-making*, that magisterial page from the life of the fields which to-day is the pride of the Luxembourg museum, and which the art of the engraver has scattered broadcast to the extent of millions of copies.

This picture represents a vast sun-bathed meadow, overstrewn with new-mown hay and punctuated, here and there, by the rounded cones of the stacks. Against the blue background of the sky, green hill-tops trace an undulant line. In the foreground a robust, bony-armed country-woman is seated on the grass, her legs stretched out before her in an attitude expressive of the utter weariness resulting from the work performed. Her head, solidly planted on her massive neck, is a marvel of realism; in her vulgar peasant face we may read health, strength, and a sort of dulled mentality born of physical fatigue. In every fibre of her exhausted body the woman is veritably resting, and through her half-parted lips it seems as though we could detect the passage of her hurried breathing. The man beside her, no less worn out than she, is stretched at full length on the thick couch of grass, and with his hat over his face, to shelter it from the sun, he is sleeping as though dead to the world.

Every detail of this canvas is perfect, because every detail is true, drawn straight from life, the fruit of minute observation. In it Bastien-Lepage once more affirms his predilection for the open country; and nothing could be more impressive than these two uncouth, vulgar, homely human beings, set amid the splendour of a meadow turned golden by the sun. It is an every-day spectacle; it would not seem at first sight to contain material for a picture. But Bastien-Lepage has succeeded in proving indisputably that beauty does not consist solely in the harmony of the body, but in the impression which emanates from scenes that are most humble in outward appearance. In these few square feet of canvas the artist has summed up, perhaps without intending it, all the majesty of nature and all the grandeur of the life of the fields. It is scarcely necessary to add that this work is a transcript of the soil of Lorraine, that good natal soil which he loved so profoundly and to which he returned eagerly, year after year.

Bastien-Lepage was exclusively the painter of the rural aspects of Lorraine; he loved its horizons, its fertile and undulating plains. And when, occasionally, he ventured into allegory, the background was still Lorraine, and the characters were developed in the familiar setting of his native village, Damvillers. And how he loved it! How he enjoyed the warm atmosphere of affection which always awaited him when his father, grandfather, and valiant and devoted "little mother" gathered at night around the family table! He made his home in Paris, because residence there was indispensable, both for business and artistic reasons; but the moment that he could escape from the capital and its constraints, he would go to rest and gather new energy in the midst of the family circle. He had a spacious studio installed in the second story of the ancestral home; and there he worked, absolutely happy so long as he could see the old grandfather at his side, pipe in mouth, examining the work with a knowing air, and the father and mother in a sort of ecstasy, as they watched him fill in his canvas.

PLATE V.—PORTRAIT OF M. HAYEM

(Museum of the Luxembourg)

A marvel of discernment and of rendering. The face, to be sure, has a strong originality; but there is no slight merit in having expressed with such striking truth the piercing intelligence of the eyes that twinkle behind the lenses of the spectacles, and the energy, tempered with satiric humour, of his whole odd physiognomy.

Nevertheless, Bastien-Lepage was no studio painter; it was not from the height of a window that he chose to contemplate nature, but in the open fields, in the very heart of the furrows; and it was there also, in the midst of the wheat and the rye, that he set up his easel and painted his peasants in action, in the daily fulfilment of their thankless task. And by picturing them thus, without artifice, in all their simplicity of gesture and coarseness of feature, he imbued his canvases with a profound spirit of poetry, through which the often brutal realism of his subjects was redeemed and ennobled. In the presence of these peasants he experienced a joy more genuine than he had ever felt before the rarest canvases in any museum. Not that he denied or disdained the genius of the great ancestors of painting; he had too much reverence for his art ever to dream of doing so. But when it came to a question of training, he could learn more from nature than from them. Listen to his own exposition of his ideas:

"What a pity," he wrote, "that we are initiated, whether we will or not, into traditions and routines, under the pretext that this is the way to train us to be artists! It would be so simple to teach the use of brush and palette, without ever once mentioning the name of Michelangelo or Raphael or Murillo or Domenichino! We could then go home, back to Brittany or Gascony, Lorraine or Normandy, and peacefully paint the portrait of our own province; and if some morning the book we had chanced to read aroused the wish to paint a Prodigal Son, or Priam at the feet of Achilles, we could reconstruct the scene to suit ourselves, without needing to resort to the museums, taking the setting from our own surroundings and making use of the models close at hand, as though the old drama dated only from yesterday. That is the way for an artist to succeed in breathing the breath of life into his art and in making it beautiful and appealing to the eyes of the whole world. And that is the goal towards which I am striving with all my strength."

As painter of the open air, he became in a certain sense the founder of a school, without meaning to be; for his conception of the painter's art won over a whole group of young artists who united in hailing him as their master. Each year his offerings to the Salon were impatiently awaited, and his followers gathered in full force before them, discussing, comparing, acclaiming; each Salon became the occasion for a new success, the critics were unanimous in praising him, the public adopted his pictures for their own, because they could understand his clear and rigorous manner. Whatever hostility he met with was among his own colleagues, at least among such of them as were discouraged and humiliated by his vigorous originality. Nevertheless, the Exposition of 1878, at which he had gathered together all his works, was an especially triumphant occasion for him; yet when the awards were distributed, he discovered that he had received nothing but a medal of the third class.

At the Salon of 1879, Bastien-Lepage exhibited his *Women gathering Potatoes*, which formed a companion piece to his *Hay-making*. Here again we have the landscape of Lorraine and the eternal and infinitely varied theme of rural labour. In a sun-parched field two women are toiling to reap the harvest of potatoes. While the one in the middle distance is stooping to turn up the ripe bulbs from the soil, the other, placed in the foreground, is striving to empty the contents of her basket into a sack which she holds open by a wonderfully natural movement of her knee. Nothing could be simpler or more humble than this subject, and yet one feels drawn towards it, conquered by the truth of these two figures, both in their attitude and their expression. Involuntarily memory conjures up another canvas, *The Gleaners*, and we realize that it is impossible to resist that higher appeal which the great artists succeed in giving to the most commonplace episode of farming life. But, unlike Millet, Bastien-Lepage does not awaken in us any compassion for these beings who toil, stooping above the earth; no touch of bitterness saddens his pictures, and the types which he shows to us have the healthy vigour of peasants who live their lives in the open air and love the soil which nourishes them.

This picture, when it appeared, produced a sensation. Coming directly after the *Hay-making*, it definitely established Bastien-Lepage's talent and placed him in the foremost rank of painters of rural life. The critics hailed this powerful canvas with enthusiasm. Théodore de Banville, writing of the Salon of 1879, said: "M. Bastien-Lepage is the king of this Exposition. Young as he is, he has started in to produce masterpieces: he is very wise! For in later years an artist continues to copy himself, with more or less cleverness and success; but the creative genius has taken wing, like a bird on whose tail we have failed to drop the indispensable grain of salt. The *October Season* pictures the harvesting of potatoes. The earth, the encompassing air as far as we can see, the sky, the solitude laden with silence, are all evoked for us in this picture by the sincerity of its powerful painter; the peasant women are done in a masterly manner, and precisely for the reason that he has seen them apart from all convention and has not tried to idealize them by any hackneyed device."

Albert Wolff was no less enthusiastic: "The colouring in *Women harvesting Potatoes* is ingratiating and discreet; not a discordant touch disturbs the beautiful harmony of this canvas, over which the silence of the open country has descended, enveloping the obscure toil. It is only artists of superior powers who can embody so much charm in a single conception."

Another feature of the same Salon was his magnificent portrait of *Madame Sarah Bernhardt*, a marvel of expression and of delicate art, embodied in a pale symphony of tenderest whites, blending harmoniously with the warmest tones of gold. The great tragic actress is portrayed draped, almost swathed, in a gown of white china silk, verging on the faintest yellowish caste; she is posed in profile, that cameo-like profile that has so often been portrayed. She is seated, with a sort of intentional rigidity, on a white fur robe, and is examining a statuette of Orpheus, in old ivory, which she holds in her hands. Her expressive and intellectual features are treated with a vigour which does full justice to the classic beauty and virile energy of the sitter.

"The work as a whole," wrote the critic of the *Revue des Beaux-Arts*, "possesses supreme distinction and an admirable delicacy of colouring. The silvery tones of the whites, the warm grays of the draped gown lead up to the freshness of the delicate, rose-like flesh tints, beneath the crown of close curled locks that seem at once massive and weightless. The artist's hand was sure of itself; it neither groped nor hesitated. The execution is such that the drawing of the gown and the lines of the face seem to have been traced by an engraver's tool. In this case, however, definiteness has not resulted in stiffness. The sharp design has not imprisoned unwilling forms; it leaves them free to move as they please within the limits of their contours which are its domain. It is worth while to examine with a lens the marvellous process which, by the aid of imperceptible half-tones, has softened the modelling of the face and hands."

PLATE VI.—PORTRAIT OF M. X——

(Museum at Verdun)

Bastien-Lepage possessed the rare quality of being able to bestow the same superior skill upon every part of a portrait. Being sincere before all else, he never tried to shirk any difficulty; this is seen in the care he took in painting the hands of all his various sitters, showing something akin to vanity in the marvellous talent he displayed in rendering them. In this portrait—just as in all the others—the hands are quite as truly a miracle of execution as the face itself.

These two pictures earned Bastien-Lepage the Cross of the Legion of Honour and a definite recognition of his talent. The artist could not keep his delight to himself and, good son that he was, wished to share it with his beloved family; so he sent for them, to pay him a visit in Paris. The grandfather and the "good little mother" arrived, full of pride in this famous son, of whom the whole world was talking. He showed them the sights of the city and was only too happy to have a chance to introduce them to his friends; he took his mother to the big shops and insisted on choosing silk cloaks and silk dresses for her. The poor woman protested, saying that they were far too fine, that she would never dare to wear anything like that. "Show us some more," ordered the devoted artist, "I want mamma to have her choice of the best there is!"

After the old people had returned home to Lorraine, Bastien-Lepage set out for England, where he was to paint the portrait of the Prince of Wales, who afterwards became King Edward VII.

In this portrait of tiny dimensions the Prince is represented in fancy costume, after the manner of Holbein. His garments recall in a measure those worn by King Henry VIII, in the celebrated portrait done by the great painter from Basle. The Collar of the Golden Fleece is displayed upon his breast. In the background of the picture may be seen dimly, through a veil of mist, the panorama of London and the gray ribbon of the Thames. The portrait is a little gem, which Bastien-Lepage wrought with the minuteness and affectedly hieratic mannerism of Holbein and the French primitive school. Although at present in possession of M. Émile Bastien-Lepage, it will eventually find its place, together with a goodly number of other canvases, in the museum of the Louvre, to which the brother of the great artist intends to bequeath them.

It should be mentioned here, in connection with this work, that Bastien-Lepage continued to make more and more of a specialty of portraits of reduced dimensions, and that he acquired in this respect a reputation of the first order. He loved these little canvases, scarcely larger than miniatures, and he expended on their scanty surfaces an inimitable skill; he embellished them with a wealth of accessory detail which brings to mind, as we look at them to-day, the formidable labours of the illuminators of the middle ages. But this goldsmith's work, far from impairing the effect of the whole, adds a certain fascination to it. And he expended upon the study of the face the same degree of devotion that he gave to the rendering of a garment. His models relive with an intensity of life such as could be expressed only by an artist who has made a life-long study of nature in her minutest manifestations.

To name over his portraits would be to mention an equal number of masterpieces. The catalogue would be too long, for Bastien-Lepage was an indefatigable workman. We may content ourselves with citing those that are most widely known: that of *M. Andrieux*, one-time Prefect of Police, whose refined features are rendered with striking truth; that of *J. Bastien-Lepage*, the artist's uncle, which is here reproduced and which shows him violin in hand, a clear and vigorous piece of brush-work, transcribing life in telling strokes, with an astonishing simplicity of means. This fine example is to be seen to-day in the museum at Verdun. And in the same museum there is still another that deserves mention; namely, the excellent *Portrait of M. X.* And we must not forget the *Portrait of André Theuriet*, born, like Bastien-Lepage, on the banks of the Meuse and attached to the painter by ties of almost fraternal affection. One feels that, in this picture, the heart must have guided the hand, for it would be difficult to find another work more magisterial in execution and more delicate in finish. And lastly, there is *Mme. Bastien-Lepage*, the "good little mother," as the great artist and loving son used to call her. He posed her in the garden of the home at Damvillers. She is seated on a stone bench; on her knees rests a large garden hat; her two hands are crossed, one over the other, and in the left she holds a little bunch of field flowers. She is clad in a loose dress of sombre colour, cut with a pelerine; and nothing but the one bright spot formed by the white collar reveals the severity of the costume. The whole attitude of the body in repose is perfect in its truth and naturalness; but our admiration changes and quickens to emotion when we raise our eyes to the level of the face of this "good little mother," a bony, irregular face, almost ugly, but so gentle, so kind, so touchingly illumined by the tender caress in the eyes as they rest upon the adored son in the course of painting her. Those emaciated features, which not even the crown of blonde hair is able to rejuvenate, are unmistakably those of a mother; if we had not known, we should inevitably have divined it; no one but a son, and a great artist as well, could have crowned the brow of a woman with such an aureole of gentleness and love.

Bastien-Lepage, whom those who envied him affected to regard as dedicated wholly to the reproduction of rustic uncouthness, had no equal in catching the radiance of feminine charms, even in their subtlest manifestations. No one was more skilled than he in seizing and recording the one particular trait, often elusive and intangible, which characterizes a woman and makes her beautiful. What delicious portraits of women we owe to him! Where could we meet with a more smiling image than that of *Mme. Godillot*, radiant and seductive, a rosy vision in the black velvet of her gown, relieved by the brilliant sheen of her white satin corsage! And what studied and elaborate art was expended on the *Portrait of Mme. Klotz*, whose magnificent brunette beauty emerges like a gorgeous lily from the surrounding whiteness of her scarf, that is all the more dazzlingly white by contrast with her sombre robe! And still again, there is the *Portrait of Mme. Juliette Drouet*, another beautiful and noble specimen of portraiture. And how marvellously Bastien-Lepage could detect the hidden soul lurking in the inmost recesses of his models and reveal it behind the transparent screen of their eyes! If Bastien-Lepage had not achieved eternal glory as an interpreter of rural life, he would still have remained celebrated as a portrait painter.

But to Bastien-Lepage portrait painting was only a side issue, a form of relaxation between two landscapes; his predilection, his one object in life, so to speak, was to return constantly to his peasants, his scenes of toil, his fields of Lorraine.

After his return from England he passed some months at Damvillers, when an impulse seized him to visit Italy, to which the verdict of a prejudiced committee had once upon a time barred his way. He proceeded straight to Venice, and it may as well be acknowledged at once, Venetian art left him cold, if not indifferent. He had never in the least understood any of the big "set pieces," and in spite of all the art of Veronese and Titian, in spite of their dazzling flare of colour, he never succeeded in understanding their sumptuous allegories or in accepting the fantastic interpretation of nature which the Venetians allowed themselves. He returned to Damvillers, profoundly disillusioned and more than ever convinced that nature alone, such as he saw it, was deserving of the attention of the true artist. There would be no object in discussing here how rightly or how ill founded such an opinion was; we note it only to indicate once more the absolute independence of the painter, his fixed determination never to imitate anyone.

And, beyond question, there is no resemblance to any other painter in that curious and remarkable picture known as *Jeanne d'Arc listening to the Voices*. Lorraine in heart and soul, Bastien-Lepage desired to pay his tribute, as so many had done before him, to the glorious heroine who, like him, had come from the banks of the Meuse. And he wished also to restore her to her natural setting, with the greatest degree of historic accuracy. Consequently it is in a Lorraine garden surrounding a Lorraine cottage that he shows us Jeanne, the shepherdess; around her are the familiar garden utensils such as peasants use to-day just as they did in the fifteenth century. She is standing in an inspired and attentive attitude, which gives to her whole countenance that forceful character which Bastien-Lepage imprints upon all his compatriots. For he wished to make her, in a certain sense, a composite type of the women of the Lorraine race, such as Theuriet has described: "The forehead low but intelligent, the eyes with drooping lids that half conceal the somewhat sullen glance; the bones prominent in cheek and jaw, the chin square, indicative of an opinionated race; the mouth large, with half parted lips, through which one perceives the passage of the deep-drawn breath." This head is always the same; under all the variations in physiognomy we always meet with the same local type: it is the head of the woman in *Hay-making* and of the *Women gathering Potatoes*, and it is also that of the "good little mother," so fundamentally and emphatically representative of Lorraine.

Nevertheless *Jeanne d'Arc listening to the Voices* was rather badly received by the critics. Without disputing the originality and vigour of the inspired shepherdess, they reproached the artist for the presence of the traditional saints. Bastien-Lepage had indicated these under the form of luminous vapour, radiating through the branches overhanging the garden: St. Michael in the golden armour of a knight of the fifteenth century, St. Margaret and St. Catherine as phantoms so diaphanous as to be hardly perceptible. The idealists complained that the picture was lacking in idealism; the realists were somewhat disconcerted to find the apparitions there at all. It must be acknowledged that Bastien-Lepage ceases to be himself the moment that he ventures to attempt the supernatural or even allegory pure and simple. He feels that he is no longer on familiar ground, he hesitates, he fumbles, and the harmony of the work suffers in consequence. Nevertheless, in spite of this undeniable defect, the face of Jeanne d'Arc will be remembered as a piece of powerful painting and genuine inspiration.

PLATE VII.—THE LITTLE CHIMNEY-SWEEP

(Collection of É. Bastien-Lepage)

This attractive picture, full of charm and vigour, belongs to the closing years of the artist's life, at the time when he was enjoying the flood tide of his talent. How much force and truth there is in this picture of the little chimney-sweep, and what graceful nimbleness in the movements of the cats that he is watching at play.

At all events, Bastien-Lepage was keenly aware of the half-way nature of his success, and from that day renounced forever the element of the marvellous and confined himself to that concrete and tangible poetry which emanates from the earth.

Some little time after his *Jeanne d'Arc*, he produced *The Mendicant*, veteran knight of the road, whose lazy life is passed in going from door to door, asking charity and compelling it if need be; suspicious looking old tramp, perhaps a thief as well, who inspires fear and whose sack is often filled through unwillingness to provoke him. The artist has pictured him with a stout stick in his hand, stowing away the slice of bread which a pretty slip of a girl in a blue apron has just given him. This fine and vigorous canvas scored almost as much of a success, at the Salon of 1881, as the admirable *Portrait of Albert Wolff*, a critic on the *Figaro* and close personal friend of the artist.

In 1882 he won a further success with his superb *Father Jacques*, a masterly study of the Lorraine peasant, and with his charming *Portrait of Mme. W.*

In 1883 came *Love in a Village*, one of his most popular canvases, in which he depicted with charming naturalness the uncomplicated and naïve courtship of rustic lovers. Here are a pair who are untroubled by curious glances; the nearer houses of the village are quite close by. Bending slightly towards his sweetheart, the man is murmuring his avowals in her ear, in a voice that, we suspect, is by no means steady. Strapping fellow that he is, he evidently lacks the habit of making pretty speeches; we can see that from the embarrassed air with which he twists his fingers. His words, however, are plainly not lacking in eloquence, for the girl, type of buxom young womanhood that we have already learned to know, has bent her head and, although her back is turned, we are sure that she is blushing as she listens to his declaration. A special atmosphere emanates from this picture, as well as that profound spirit of poetry which is inseparable from the eternal song of love.

HIS PREMATURE END

At this period Bastien-Lepage had already begun to incur the first attacks of the disease which was destined so soon to end his days. He suffered violent pains in the kidneys. He became melancholy, nervous, irritable; he shut himself up in his studio in the Rue Legendre, and even his best friends could not gain admittance. The doctors who were called in recognized the gravity of his illness and ordered energetic treatment and a change of air. The poor artist reconciled himself to go for a time to Brittany, and his choice fell on Concarneau. The keen sea air produced a temporary betterment, and he took advantage of it to work, for he could not resign himself to lay aside his palette and brushes. He spent entire days in a boat and, in spite of his sufferings, executed several landscapes of rare beauty. But his condition, instead of improving, took a turn for the worse. "The digestive tube," he wrote to Theuriet, "is always kicking up a row!" The pain in the kidneys and bowels became at this time so violent that he was forced to decide to return to Paris, in order to consult the men of science once again.

This time, when Dr. Potain examined him, he could no longer deceive himself as to the artist's fate; he saw that his patient was irremediably condemned. However, a sojourn in a milder climate might prolong his life for a few months; so he advised Algeria. The prospect of the journey, the desire to make the acquaintance of this land of sunshine which Delacroix, Decamps, and Fromentin had taught him to love, for a few days gave a false strength to the poor sufferer, which produced a deceptive appearance of renewed health and even deceived the artist himself. Besides, Mme. Bastien-Lepage, the "good little mother," was to accompany him, and this unselfish and tender devotion warmed his heart. The poor woman forced back her tears in order to smile upon the unfortunate son whom she knew to be doomed. And so the pitiful pair set forth for the land of sunshine, she consumed with grief, and he almost joyous in the hope of a speedy cure.

His first letters to his friends bore the imprint of good spirits; Algeria aroused his enthusiasm by its clear and vibrant colours; his disease declared a brief truce and he began to form projects. The thought of dying had not yet even vaguely occurred to him, though, for that matter, he had no fear of death. The previous year he had painted *Gambetta on his Death-bed*; and his frequent visits to Ville-d'Avray led him to discuss the inevitable end of life. "I am not afraid of death," he said, "dying is nothing,—the important thing is to survive oneself, and who can be sure of establishing a claim upon posterity? But there! I am talking nonsense! So long as our work is true, nothing else matters."

But before long the ravages of the disease began to make headway; the kidneys no longer performed their function, and he suffered atrocious agonies which stretched him for days at a time on his back. Even the burning heat of the African sun no longer had strength enough to animate his shattered physique; the brush, which the artist from time to time still attempted to take up, fell from between his fingers. He, Bastien-Lepage, painter of the soil, found himself unable to transfer to canvas the enchantment of that land of fairy tale! And he poured forth his distress in long and poignant letters, in which could be read in every line the loss of hope and the sure prevision of the now inevitable end.

PLATE VIII.—THE ARTIST'S UNCLE

(Museum at Verdun)

Here is still another kindly and vigorous face from Lorraine, forcefully modelled, with salient jaw bones, betraying the obstinacy of the race. An air of good nature softens the energy of this face, and the eyes sparkle with intelligence. This portrait is treated in a free-handed manner, with unfaltering strokes, and its colouring is especially excellent.

As no amelioration took place, Bastien-Lepage made the return journey to Paris towards the end of May, 1884. He went back to his studio in the Rue Legendre, where he had formerly passed such happy hours in the full enjoyment of a talent at its zenith and a constitution apparently able to defy all tests. Now, however, he dragged around a dying body, with disease gnawing at his vitals. He could no longer sleep without the aid of powerful doses of morphine. The winter-time increased his suffering; his strength rapidly failed him; and, on the tenth of December, at six o'clock in the evening, he drew his last breath, at the age of thirty-six years.

As long as he could hold a brush, Bastien-Lepage continued to work, in spite of the sufferings which racked him. During the year preceding his death, while he was already experiencing frightful tortures, he painted *The Woman making Lye* and *The Little Chimney-sweep*, the latter of which is here reproduced. This admirable canvas is to be seen now at the studio of the painter's brother at Neuilly, and forms part of the legacy which M. Émile Bastien-Lepage intends to bequeath to the Louvre. It has never been shown at any Salon, and for that matter there are a good many other paintings and portraits which have never been exhibited in public and which are not for that reason any the less remarkable. We may cite at random: *The Portrait of M. É. Bastien-Lepage, The Prince of Wales, Mme. Juliette Drouet, A Little Girl going to School, The Little Pedler asleep, The Vintage, No Help! The Thames at London,* etc.

The very year of his death, shortly before his departure for Algeria, Bastien-Lepage executed a delicious little canvas entitled *The Forge*, in which the artist expended a surprising amount of talent and skill, and which enables us to realize what extraordinary heights his ever progressive genius might have attained, but for the blind and brutal cruelty of Destiny.

His death was a time of mourning for the arts; the regrets which he left behind him were unanimous. Even those who had been opposed to his aesthetic creed paid homage to his great conscientiousness as an artist and his noble character as a man.

During March and April, 1885, only a few months after his death, all literary and artistic Paris flocked to the Hotel de Chimay, an adjunct to the École des Beaux-Arts, where a posthumous exhibition of his works had been organized.

At this exhibition the entire body of his works had been brought together. The museums had loaned the canvases which they possessed and the private collectors had done their share towards the glorification of the artist by entrusting to the organizers a goodly number of paintings and portraits which had never figured in any of the Salons.

Thus it was made possible to comprehend at a single glance the life-work of this remarkable artist and to appreciate the distance he had traversed, the progress he had made during his brief existence, and the brilliant prospects that were destroyed by his untimely death.

From all these numerous works, exhibited side by side, what stood out most clearly was the unity of thought which had conceived them and the dogged fidelity to principles which had controlled their execution. At the same time they revealed the amazing adaptability of his talent, which essayed the most diverse and conflicting subjects with the same realistic vigour, bestowing even upon his vaporous and delicate portraits of women a touch which, while light, is unmistakably his own, and in which we recognize that noble, conscientious workmanship, free from all artifice, which was the distinctive hall-mark both of his painting and of his character.

But the quality which dominates all the rest in the work of Bastien-Lepage, and which emanates from it like the fragrance which is exhaled by certain precious essences, is his ardent and deep-rooted love for his native soil. This form of local patriotism, determined by the boundaries of Lorraine, underwent a noble expansion to the point of encircling the entire earth; for while the painter chose his models out of the familiar landscape of his childhood's home, his observation and his art broke out of the bounds of this special setting and embraced rustic humanity throughout France and even beyond. His peasants are unmistakably from the banks of the Meuse in type and in customs, but they are from the world at large in gesture and in philosophy of life. Whether he comes from the North or from the South, the tiller of the soil wages the same conflict with ungrateful furrows, the spade and the plough imprint the same calluses on his bony hands, the sun browns his energetic and stubborn features to the same deep tan. It is in this respect that the art of Bastien-Lepage assumes a higher significance; like Millet, it is not a peasant whom he paints, but the peasant, forever unchanging in spite of latitude. But if his work has attained this higher eminence of generalization, it is precisely for the reason that the artist's watchful eye has succeeded in discovering, in the life of the peasantry, that state of mind which is common to them all, that immutable gesture which they have always made and always will make. He has understood and translated with inspired eloquence their rugged strength, their naïve awkwardness, their simple intelligence.

Another glorious distinction of Bastien-Lepage was that he loved the fields as well as he loved the peasants. Not fields drowned beneath melancholy shadow and pallid shifting light, but fields bathed in sunshine, until the golden tassels of the grain crackle like sparks under the fire of the midday sun. Always and everywhere he sought for light, and in the midst of it his modest protagonists of rustic life stand out in all their vigour.

It would be easy to cite, among our best contemporary painters, a considerable number of artists who are brilliantly continuing the tradition left by Bastien-Lepage and emulating his predilection for the luminous brilliance of the open air. How often, in the presence of a canvas by Lhermitte, our thoughts go back to the painter of Lorraine, whose vigorous execution and joyous colouring seem to have been reincarnated! Art is indebted to Bastien-Lepage for having reinstated nature in all her literal truth by proving that, in order to be beautiful, she has no need of artificial and superfluous adornment.

Lorraine, out of gratitude, wished to perpetuate the memory of this glorious son of the Meuse, who had so eloquently celebrated the vitality and poetry of his natal earth. It was at Damvillers itself that it was decided to raise a monument to the great painter; and around its pedestal there were gathered the "good little mother," all in tears, the assembled population of the village and the whole region round about, and even the Government took part in the pious ceremony by sending as its representative M. Gustave Larroumet, director of the Beaux-Arts. This eloquent art critic brought as a tribute to the departed painter the official seal of immortality, and he pronounced it in terms vibrant with emotion.

"At the moment," he said, "when ordinarily the best of artists have done no more than to give indications of their originality and when ripening years alone begin to keep the promises of youth, Jules Bastien-Lepage died, leaving masterpieces behind him, besides having liberated an artistic formula from the tendencies and exaggerations which hampered it, and indicated to the art of painting a new pathway along which his young heirs are advancing with an assured step. He loved nature and truth; he loved his own people, and no one ever lived who was surrounded with a greater degree of affection; he inspired faithful friendships which he himself enjoyed to the full; and those whom he left behind soothe their heart-ache with the balm of tender memories; he practised his art without ever making sacrifice to passing fashion or sordid profit; there was no place in his mind or in his heart for any other than noble and generous thoughts. Let us comfort ourselves, therefore, for what his death has taken from us by the thought of what his life has left to us, and let us assign him his place in the ranks of the younger master painters who have been mown down in full flower, close beside that of Géricault and of Henri Regnault."

In his admirable biographic and critical study of Bastien-Lepage, whose personal friend he had been, M. L. de Fourcaud, by way of conclusion, bids him this touching farewell:

"Poor Bastien-Lepage, snatched away one winter's night, at thirty-six years of age, in the fairest flowering of his bright promise, in the richest expansion of his personality; may each returning month of May bring at least an abundance of blossoms to the apple tree beside his grave! For the blossoms of the apple were always, in his eyes, so fair a sight!"

To-day he sleeps forever in a corner of that Lorraine land which he loved so dearly, and perhaps in the cemetery of his native village his shade can still hear the familiar accents of his native dialect. The great painter of Lorraine could never have slept his eternal sleep in any other soil than that.

Painter of flowers, painter of nature, painter of the earth which is forever deathless and forever renewed, Bastien-Lepage has chosen that better part; his work will live as long as these, his models, and will go down through the centuries in all the splendour of increasing beauty and eternal youth.

Lector House believes that a society develops through a two-fold approach of continuous learning and adaptation, which is derived from the study of classic literary works spread across the historic timeline of literature records. Therefore, we aim at reviving, repairing and redeveloping all those inaccessible or damaged but historically as well as culturally important literature across subjects so that the future generations may have an opportunity to study and learn from past works to embark upon a journey of creating a better future.

This book is a result of an effort made by Lector House towards making a contribution to the preservation and repair of original ancient works which might hold historical significance to the approach of continuous learning across subjects.

HAPPY READING & LEARNING!

LECTOR HOUSE LLP
E-MAIL: lectorpublishing@gmail.com